CW01432536

James Bentley is a personal injury and clinical negligence barrister based at Guildhall Chambers in Bristol. He has a busy practice that stretches across a wide range of matters, and is regularly instructed by both claimants and defendants in cases that involve allegations of fundamental dishonesty.

A Practical Guide to QOCS and Fundamental Dishonesty

A Practical Guide to QOCS and Fundamental Dishonesty

James Bentley,
Barrister,
Guildhall Chambers

Law Brief Publishing

© James Bentley

All rights reserved. No part of this publication may be reproduced, stored in a retrieval system, or transmitted, in any form or by any means, electronic, mechanical, photocopying, recording or otherwise, without the prior permission of the publisher.

Excerpts from judgments and statutes are Crown copyright. Any Crown Copyright material is reproduced with the permission of the Controller of OPSI and the Queen's Printer for Scotland. Some quotations may be licensed under the terms of the Open Government Licence (http://www.nationalarchives.gov.uk/doc/open-government-licence/version/3).

Cover image © iStockphoto.com/BernardaSv

The information in this book was believed to be correct at the time of writing. All content is for information purposes only and is not intended as legal advice. No liability is accepted by either the publisher or author for any errors or omissions (whether negligent or not) that it may contain. Professional advice should always be obtained before applying any information to particular circumstances.

Published 2017 by Law Brief Publishing, an imprint of Law Brief Publishing Ltd
30 The Parks
Minehead
Somerset
TA24 8BT

www.lawbriefpublishing.com

Paperback: 978-1-911035-31-2

To my wife Rebecca,

who is always striving to

keep me honest!

PREFACE

When the phrase 'fundamental dishonesty' was introduced, there followed a huge flurry of articles, seminars, papers and the like, all about what 'fundamental dishonesty' might mean, and how it would (or should) be applied.

Despite all that 'excitement', and whilst there are many authoritative cases on dishonesty generally, we are still yet to receive any guidance from the appellate courts on fundamental dishonesty specifically.

What therefore follows in this book is largely (although not entirely) a collection of County Court decisions and other such cases involving dishonesty. Whilst such cases are not authoritative, they nevertheless reflect the current approach that District and Circuit Judges take when asked to adjudicate on such matters. The rest, I am afraid, is based simply on my opinions and experience, and which you are of course perfectly entitled to ignore!

The book states the law as at the 24th October 2017.

James Bentley
October 2017

CONTENTS

CHAPTER ONE
BRIEF REASONS FOR A COSTS SHIFTING REGIME

Qualified one-way costs shifting was one of the many reforms that followed on from Lord Justice Jackson's extensive review into the cost of civil litigation. The review was aimed primarily at bringing the overall cost of civil litigation down in the fairest way possible. There were concerns that the costs of civil litigation had become too high, and so the Government was of the view that clearly something had to be done. As the Lord Chancellor opined (in a speech cited at the beginning of Lord Justice Jackson's preliminary report):

> "*I am concerned about another element of legal services –*
> "*No win – no fee" arrangements. It's claimed they have*
> *provided greater access to justice, but the behaviour of some*
> *lawyers in ramping up their fees in these cases is nothing*
> *short of scandalous.*"[1]

It wasn't just the fact that litigation was so expensive that was so scandalous. As far as the public mood was concerned, it might be fair to say that most were outraged that those

---

1 LJ Jackson's preliminary review, paragraph 1.3

expenses were being incurred in pursuit of cases that were deemed to be (for want of a better word) 'unattractive'.

As a result, ATE premiums came under heavy scrutiny. Prior to the Jackson reforms, such premiums often came at a heavy price. The number of policies being issued increased sharply after April 2000 (which coincided with the time from which such premiums became recoverable from the losing party). Lord Justice Jackson's view, as articulated again within his preliminary report, was that the recoverability of premiums was twofold:

'Defendants end up bearing their own costs of all cases in that area, regardless of the outcome of any individual case. In those cases which defendants lose they bear their own costs in the ordinary way. In those cases which defendants win, they nominally recover their costs, but they pay in full for that privilege by reason of their liability for ATE premiums in many other cases.'

'The second effect of recoverable premiums in any area where ATE insurance is the norm is also plain. The claimants' disbursements of all cases in that area are trans-ferred from claimants to defendants, regardless of the

outcome of any individual case. In those cases which they win, claimants get their disbursements under the "loser pays" rule. In those cases which they lose, claimants get their disbursements through the mechanism of recoverable ATE premiums in other cases.[2]

Regrettably, market forces had done little to bring the cost of such premiums down. As Lord Hoffman bemoaned in <u>Callery v Gray (Nos 1 and 2) [2002] UKHL 28</u>, the only restraint upon the cost of premiums was the power of the costs Judge to reduce that premium on assessment. However, in practice it was inevitable that the Judge would lack any criteria to assess the reasonableness of a premium by, and it was often extremely difficult for the paying party to success-fully challenge the premium on detailed assessment.

However, whilst the costs of ATE premiums were a problem, even the most trenchant of critics had to acknowledge (as the Lord Chancellor did) that they had one major benefit, namely that they increased access to justice without placing a burden on the public purse. The question was therefore: how did one get rid of the cost of premiums but retain its benefits?

---

2 LJ Jackson's preliminary review, Chapter 47, 3.4 to 3.5

CHAPTER TWO
QUALIFIED ONE-WAY COSTS
SHIFTING ('QOCS')

Before exploring the qualifications to one-way costs shifting, it will be useful to first look at when the QOCS regime does and does not apply.

<u>The substantive scope of the QOCS provisions</u>

<u>*CPR 44.13*</u> reads as follows:

(1) This Section applies to proceedings which include a claim for damages—

(a) For personal injuries;

(b) Under the Fatal Accidents Act 1976; or

(c) Which arises out of death or personal injury and survives for the benefit of an estate by virtue of section 1(1) of the Law Reform (Miscellaneous Provisions) Act 1934,

But does not apply to applications pursuant to Section 33 of the Senior Courts Act 1981 or section 52 of the County Courts Act 1984 (applications for pre-action disclosure), or where rule 44.17 applies.

(2) In this Section, "claimant" means a person bringing a claim to which this Section applies or an estate on behalf of which such a claim is brought, and includes a person making a counterclaim or an additional claim.

Claim for 'damages for personal injuries'

Wagenaar v Weekend Travel Limited t/s Ski Weekend [2014] EWCA Civ 1105, was one of the first and indeed, one of the few times the Court of Appeal have had the opportunity to review the qualified one way costs shifting provisions.

The claimant had booked a package holiday to go skiing in Chamonix. Unfortunately, whilst on holiday, she was involved in an accident, and suffered injuries as a result. As such, she pursued the first defendant for compensation under the Package Travel Regulations. The first defendant in turn pursued the ski instructor by way of a Part 20 claim for an indemnity/contribution, alleging that if the accident was caused by anybody's negligence, it was hers (i.e. the instructor's).

The claim against the first defendant was dismissed, as was the first defendant's Part 20 claim against the instructor. When it came to costs the trial Judge (HHJ Hughes QC) made the following order:

(a) The claimant should pay the defendant's costs, but that such an order was not to be enforced against the claimant pursuant to the provisions of CPR 44.13 and CPR 44.14; and

(b) The defendant should pay the third party's costs, but that such an order was not to be enforced against the claimant pursuant to the provisions of CPR 44.13 and CPR 44.14

The instructor appealed, submitting that the Judge had erred in finding that QOCS applied to the Part 20 proceedings.

The key wording to focus on was 'a claim for damages *for personal injuries.*' A Part 20 claim was a claim not for personal injuries, but for a contribution or indemnity. That conclusion not only made sense as a matter of construction, but also in so far as it would be illogical if Part 20 claimants and defendants could recover their costs. As Lord Justice Vos pointed out, that was not the purpose of the QOCS regime:

> *"Suffice it to say that the rationale for QOCS that Sir Rupert Jackson expressed in those sections came through loud and clear. It was that QOCS was a way of protecting those who had suffered injuries from the risk of facing adverse costs orders obtained by insured or self-insured parties or well-funded defendants. It was, Sir Rupert thought, far preferable to the previous regime of recoverable success fees under CFAs and recoverable ATE premiums. There is nothing in the Jackson Report that supports the idea that QOCS might apply to the costs of disputes between those liable to the injured parties as to how those personal injury damages should be funded amongst themselves."[1]*

The court was fortified in that view by looking at some practical examples. In medical negligence cases for example:

---

1 See paragraph 36 of Wagenaar

"...a claimant may sue a doctor, a health authority and the manufacturer of some piece of medical equipment. It would be strange if there could be no costs orders enforced between the defendants at the end of a long battle in the cross-contribution claims between them where it was ultimately proved that the doctor and the health authority were blameless but the injury was caused by a defective piece of medical equipment. In such a case, the claimant's damages might be agreed, and the argument might be almost wholly between the defendants – or possibly third parties, if any of them were not originally sued.

"In road traffic cases, the typical situation is equally revealing. Injured passengers in a car may sue the driver of the car in which they are injured. That driver may seek to pass on the blame in CPR Part 20 proceedings to any number of other insured parties, such as another driver involved in the collision, or a local authority responsible for maintenance of the road. Again, there might be little argument as to the claimant's entitlement for damages, but significant dispute between the insured parties as to who was to blame. It would be surprising if there could be no effective costs orders made between defendants in their contribution claims (if there was ultimately more than one)

and between defendants and the third parties in the additional claims made."[2]

The message from the Court of Appeal was therefore clear – the QOCS regime will apply to claims for personal injury only, and not to claims for a contribution or indemnity.

Other statutory claims

A separate question from the one posed in *Wagenaar* was whether or not QOCS could apply to statutory claims such as, for example, claims against the MIB.

The question of whether QOCS applied to MIB claims was specifically addressed in *Howe v Motor Insurers' Bureau [2017] EWCA Civ 932*, where the facts were as follows.

Mr. Howe was severely injured as a result of an accident whilst driving in France. A wheel had come off from a lorry and had collided with his lorry. However, it was impossible to identify the lorry from which the wheel came, or its driver, or its insurer. His claim was therefore pursued under *Regulation*

---

2 See paragraphs 41 and 42

13 of the Motor Vehicles (Compulsory Insurance) (Information Centre and compensation Board) Regulations 2003.

Unfortunately for Mr. Howe, the claim was dismissed on the grounds of limitation. The defendant pursued their costs, averring that the claimant could not avail himself of the protection provided by the qualified one-way costs shifting provisions in CPR 44.13. The claim, it was submitted, was based upon the Regulations and was not therefore a claim for '*damages for personal injuries*'.

At first instance, the Judge (Mr. Justice Stewart) held that:

> "*The rationale for QOCS can be said to extend to a claimant in Mr. Howe's position. He comes fairly and squarely within the citations which I have set out above in paragraph 11, subject to whether, in relation to the Jackson report citation this is 'personal injuries litigation'. He is a person who has suffered personal injuries and, absent QOCS, he faces enforcement of the adverse costs order obtained by the MIB, which is a well-funded defendant. If his claim does not have QOCS protection, then injured*

persons in situations similar to his may be deterred from
bringing claims for compensation."[3]

However, and despite that acknowledgment, the Judge
continued:

"*The substance of the claim is based on the MIB's liability*
to compensate the claimant under Regulation 13 of the
2003 Regulations. As I found, on the way the case was
argued before me and pleaded, this is a claim under statute
(judgment paragraph 82)..."[4]

"*I was not addressed in any detail about the meaning of*
damages, nor was I taken to any authority on something
which has caused problems in previous cases. I have
however reminded myself of certain passages in McGregor
on Damages 19th Edition which makes it clear that
damages are simply an award in money for a civil wrong
and that, to retain the requirement of a wrong is entirely
necessary, this being the essential feature of damages; actions
claiming money under statute, where the claim is made

---

3 See paragraph 13

4 See paragraph 15

independently of a wrong, are not actions for damages. (Paragraphs 1-001, 1-004, 1-007).

There being no breach of duty alleged against the MIB or any other wrong alleged against them, it seems to me diffi-cult to conclude that a claim based on regulation 13 is a claim within the meaning of Rule 44.13."[5]

The claimant appealed. The issues on appeal were whether:

(a) The EU principles of equivalence and effectiveness were engaged in relation to the CPR.

(b) Reference in CPR 44.13 to "damages for personal injuries" could be interpreted, comfortably within the Marleasing principles, to include a claim for compensation under reg.13; and

(c) The appellant had claimed a sum that was "due and owing" under the Regulations.

It was held that national rules such as the CPR had to be interpreted so as to be compatible with the objective of the

---

5 See paragraph 16

Directive, which meant giving effect to the principles of equivalence and effectiveness. That principle meant putting the claimant into an equivalent position to those who were claiming against an identifiable and insured driver.

Whilst it was true that the strict interpretation of the word *'damages'* meant that there had to be some type of breach of duty, the word "damages" could be treated as including 'compensation' as per the Regulation, which did not go against the grain of the CPR. Indeed, as was noted at first instance, the glossary of terms in Appendix E to the CPR itself described *"damages'* as a *"sum of money awarded by the court as compensation to the claimant'*.

The appeal was therefore allowed, and QOCS will therefore apply to MIB claims also.

Mixed claims

Questions have been raised as to the application of QOCS where a claimant seeks several different remedies, only one of which is a claim for damages for personal injuries. Although this was not explicitly in issue in _Wagenaar_ the Court nevertheless did touch upon the subject of 'mixed claims':

> "_It is true, however, that the word "proceedings" in CPR Rule 44.13 is a wide word which could, in theory, include the entire umbrella of the litigation in which commercial parties dispute responsibility for the payment of personal injury damages. I do not think that would be an appropriate construction. Instead, I think the word "proceedings" in CPR Part 44.13 was used because the QOCS regime is intended to catch claims for damages for personal injuries, where other claims are made in addition by the same claimant. There may, for example, in the ordinary road traffic claim, be claims for damaged property in addition to the claim for personal injury damages, and the draftsman would plainly not have wished to allow such additional matters to take the claim outside the QOCS regime._
>
> _Thus, in my judgment, CPR Rule 44.13 is applying QOCS to a single claim against a defendant or defendants, which includes a claim for damages for personal injuries or the other claims specified in CPR Rule 44.13(1)(b) and (c), but may also have other claims brought by the same claimant within that single claim. Argument has not been_

addressed to the question of whether QOCS should apply to a subsidiary claim for damages not including damages for personal injuries made by such a claimant against another defendant in the same action as the personal injury claim. I would prefer to leave that question to a case in which it arises. CPR Rule 44.13 is not applying QOCS to the entire action in which any such claim for damages for personal injuries or the other claims specified in CPR Rule 44.13(1) (b) and (c) is made."[6]

In <u>*Robert Jeffreys v the Commissioner of the Police of the Metropolis (Mr. Justice Morris QC, QBD, 4th May 2017, unreported)*</u> the claimant brought a claim against the police following his arrest for: assault, false imprisonment, misfeasance in public office and malicious prosecution. He claimed exemplary and aggravated damages, and alleged that he had suffered pain, distress, anxiety, loss of liberty and (most importantly for our purposes) soft tissue injuries to his hands.

The Judge at first instance held that at the heart of the claim were the allegations of misfeasance, and that the personal injury claim was simply ancillary to that. As such, any costs

---

6 See paragraphs 39 and 40

order made could be enforced to the extent of 70% of the sum.

CPR 44.16 (2) (b) allowed for costs orders to be enforced where the claim, *'was made for the benefit of the claimant other than a claim to which this section applies.'* It was held on appeal that the claimant had sought substantial damages *other* than those for personal injury (namely for loss of liberty, fear and upset) and that therefore there could be an enforceable costs order that represented the proportion of the claim that was not for personal injuries.

If *Jeffries* is to be followed, one must look at the damages claimed, and what proportion of them arise out of personal injury and what proportion do not. After that apportionment, a percentage based costs order may be made.

Temporal scope

As far as any temporal scope applies, it is well known that if there is a pre-commencement funding arrangement in place (i.e. a CFA signed before the 1st April 2013) then the QOCS provisions will not apply.[7]

In most cases it will be self-evident as to whether such a funding arrangement is in place (either it is or it isn't). That said, there are instances where the picture is more complicated. For example, what is the situation where there is both a pre-commencement funding arrangement *and* a post-commencement funding arrangement? That was the case in *Catalano v Espley-Tyas Development Group Ltd [2017] EWCA Civ 1132*.

In *Catalano* the claimant had made a claim for NIHL (Noise Induced Hearing Loss) and began proceedings under a CFA dated the 13th June 2012. However, ATE insurance was declined. After obtaining expert evidence, the claimant then entered into a second CFA with the same solicitors, this time dated the 15th July 2013. The claim was discontinued one day before trial. The Judge held that she could not benefit from QOCS. The claimant appealed.

The Court of Appeal dismissed the appeal. Firstly, the words 'a funding arrangement' did not mean 'an un-terminated'

---

7 See CPR 44.17

funding arrangement. That would be reading words into the rules that were not there. Secondly, such an approach would be absurd. As the Court pointed out, if it the claimant were right then:

> "*A claimant could make an agreement providing for a success fee and purchase ATE insurance and wait until shortly before trial to re-assess his or her prospects. If they appeared to be high, such claimant could continue and claim the cost of the ATE premium and the success fee as costs from the defendants; if they appeared to be low, he or she could cancel the original CFA, make a second CFA and then discontinue the claim a day later and escape the costs consequences. The framers of the rules could not have intended that a claimant should be able to blow hot and cold in that way.*"[8]

Appeals

The issue of whether QOCS continues to apply to appeals was decided in *Parker v Butler [2016] EWHC 1251 (QB)*.

---

8 Paragraph 24

The claimant failed in his claim for personal injuries. He appealed, and although he was granted permission, the appeal was dismissed. Although the provisions clearly restrict QOCS to claims for damages for personal injuries, the question in _Parker_ was whether that claim included the subsequent appeal.

Mr. Justice Edis held that:

> "*An appeal by a claimant against the dismissal of his claim for personal injuries is a means of pursuing that claim against the defendant or defendants who succeeded in defeating that claim at trial. There is no difference between the parties or the relief sought as there is between the original claim and the Part 20 claim. Most importantly, to my mind there is no difference between the nature of the claimant at trial and the appellant on appeal. He is the same person, and the QOCS regime exists for his benefit as the best way to protect his access to justice to pursue a personal injury claim. To construe the word "proceedings" as excluding an appeal which was necessary if he were to succeed in establishing the claim which had earlier*

attracted costs protection would do nothing to serve the purpose of the QOCS regime."[9]

QOCS protection therefore continues throughout the appeals process.

Summary

In short, and by way of re-cap:

- For QOCS to apply the claim must be for compensation for personal injuries, rather than for any other remedy (e.g. contribution).

- In MIB claims, 'damages' can be taken to mean 'compensation' as per the Regulations, thereby affording QOCS protection to claimants.

- In mixed claims, the court may look at what proportion of the damages arise out of personal injuries and what proportion do not.

---

9 See paragraph 17

- If the proceedings are funded by a CFA signed before the 1st April 2013, then the provisions do not apply.

- The word 'proceedings' includes any appeals in the substantive matter, but probably does not include any proceedings or appeals relating to costs.

CHAPTER THREE
THE MEANING OF FUNDAMENTAL DISHONESTY

The origins of CPR 44.16

One could not abolish the recoverability of ATE premiums, and simply put an unadulterated cost shifting regime in its place. Clearly therefore, if cost shifting was to replace the recoverability of ATE premiums, then the regime had to make sure that there was not any type of 'carte blanche' protection for claimants. The debate then became one of what that (or those) qualification(s) should be.

Interestingly, the term *'fundamental dishonesty'* is not mentioned once, in either Lord Justice Jackson's preliminary report or within his final report. When it came to suggesting the qualifications to his proposed costs-shifting regime, the suggestion within the preliminary report was that the power to enforce a costs order should be exercised only in *'exceptional circumstances'.*[1] Although those circumstances were not specified, it was clear that the provisions needed to make sure that QOCS didn't provide an incentive for and indeed should

---

1 Jackson LJ, preliminary report page 226

actively deter '*frivolous claims*[2]. As such, Lord Justice Jackson recommended that:

> "*The claimant must be at risk of some adverse costs, in order to deter (a) frivolous claims and (b) frivolous applications in the course of otherwise reasonable litigation. In my view, the best formula is that contained in section 11(1) of the 1999 Act. This provides a proper degree of protection against adverse costs without eliminating all personal risk. It is a formula which is tried and tested, having been included in all legal aid legislation since the original Legal Aid and Advice Act 1949.*"

For those unfamiliar with the Access to Justice Act 1999, the section referred to above states that:

> "*S. 11 (1) Except in prescribed circumstances, costs ordered against an individual in relation to any proceedings or part of proceedings funded for him shall not exceed the amount (if any) which is a reasonable one for him to pay having regard to all the circumstances including—*

---

2 Jackson LJ, final report page 189

(a) the financial resources of all the parties to the proceedings, and

(b) their conduct in connection with the dispute to which the proceedings relate; and

for this purpose proceedings, or a part of proceedings, are funded for an individual if services relating to the proceedings or part are funded for him by the Commission as part of the Community Legal Service."

The wording recommended by Lord Justice Jackson was therefore identical:

"Costs ordered against the claimant in any claim for personal injuries or clinical negligence shall not exceed the amount (if any) which is a reasonable one for him to pay having regard to all the circumstances including:

(a) The financial resources of all the parties to the proceedings, and

(b) Their conduct in connection with the dispute to which the proceedings relate."[3]

Whilst the wording of the specific provisions would be a matter for the Civil Procedure Rule Committee, the above provision would nevertheless allow the court to make an enforceable costs order:

"(a) Where the claimant has behaved unreasonably (e.g. bringing a frivolous or fraudulent claim);

(b) Where the defendant is neither insured nor a large organisation which is self-insured; or

(c) Where the claimant is conspicuously wealthy."[4]

It is interesting to note how wide the *'exceptional circumstances'* provisions could have been, and that they could have not only excluded frivolous claims, but also cases where the claimant had the means to pay for litigation out of his or her own pocket. If more regard had been had to the third exception (financial resources) then would it be possible that the

---

3 Jackson LJ's final report at 4.7

4 Jackson LJ's final report at 4.8

QOCS provisions would not apply to claims funded by before the event legal expenses insurance? Or to anybody else who happen to be 'of means'? Perhaps the view was taken that by creating fewer exceptions; there would be less satellite litigation – a proposition that is almost certainly true.

The definition

There is no definition of the term '*fundamental dishonesty*' either within the rules or the practice direction to CPR 44. There is the same lack of definition within Section 57 of the Criminal Justice and Courts Act 2015. The Minister for Justice (Lord Faulks), who was responsible for seeing that legislation through Parliament explained that:

> "*An adverb to qualify a concept such as dishonesty is not linguistically attractive, but if we ask a jury to decide a question such as dishonesty, or ask a judge to decide whether someone has been fundamentally dishonest, it is well within the capacity of any judge. They will know exactly what the clause is aimed at—not the minor inaccuracy about bus fares or the like, but something that goes*

to the heart. I do not suggest that it wins many prizes for elegance, but it sends the right message to the judge."

He added:

"The sanction imposed by the clause is a serious one—denial of compensation to which prima facie somebody is entitled—and we believe that it should be imposed only where it goes to the heart of a claim."[5]

In relation to CPR 44.16, we know that the lack of definition was in fact entirely deliberate. In his third implementation lecture Lord Justice Jackson said:

"What conduct will deprive the claimant of costs protection? This issue is discussed in the workshop materials. I agree that if the claimant's claim is fraudulent or is struck out as an abuse of process, the claimant should forfeit costs protection. However, I do not believe that either litigants or the court will be assisted by a practice direction which gives guidance on borderline cases. Any such guidance is likely to generate increased satellite litigation for the reasons set out

---

5 Hansard, 23/07/14, Lords, Column 1268

in para. 2.3 above. There is a whole costs bar out there just waiting to sink its teeth into the new provisions."[6]

Nevertheless, and in the absence of any guidance, Judges at the County Court level have now become (relatively) used to dealing with the concept.

Dishonesty

Sometimes it will be obvious that the claim was dishonest. As the Judge in *Menary v Darnton (13th December 2016, Portsmouth CC, HHJ Hughes QC)* commented:

> *"The use of the word 'dishonesty' in the present context necessarily imports well understood and ordinary concepts of deceit, falsity and deception. In essence, it is the advancing of a claim without an honest and genuine belief in its truth."*[7]

In many instances (such as in *Menary*) the dishonesty will be obvious. In that case, the claimant (driving his Vauxhall

---

6 Paragraph 4.3

7 See paragraph 10 of Menary

Astra) stopped at a junction so as to allow a car to enter the main road. It was alleged that the defendant (on his motorbike) proceeded to drive into the rear of the claimant's vehicle, and as a result, that he suffered personal injury. The defendant's case was that there was no collision at all.

The first instance Judge agreed with the defendant that there was no collision, but declined to make a finding of fundamental dishonesty. Unsurprisingly, on appeal, HHJ Hughes QC asked rhetorically; if there was no collision, and that was not dishonest, then what is? The dishonesty was obvious.

Where the dishonesty is so obvious, it is clear that a working definition will be of little assistance.

However, in cases that are not so obvious, there is still merit in seeking to grasp what a working definition of dishonesty would look like. In doing so, it is submitted that it may be helpful to look at the test for the tort of fraudulent misrepresentation (otherwise known as deceit).

The conditions for establishing fraudulent misrepresentation were established in *Derry v Peek [1886–90] All ER Rep 1 at 22*:

'*… fraud is proved when it is shown that a false representation has been made (1) knowingly, or (2) without belief in its truth, or (3) recklessly, careless whether it be true or false.' (per Lord Herschell.)*'

In *Standard Chartered Bank v Pakistan National Shipping Corp and others (No 2) [2000] 1 All. E. R. (Comm)*[8] the Court of Appeal confirmed therefore that:

"*It is not necessary that the maker of the statement was 'dishonest' as that word is used in the criminal law. The relevant intention is that the false statement shall be acted upon by a person to whom it is addressed. If the false statement was made knowingly and that intention is proved, then the basis for liability for the tort of deceit is established.*"[9]

It is submitted that the criteria for the tort of deceit is as good a starting point as any for attempting to more clearly define 'dishonesty' within the context of CPR 44.16. On that basis, one must show that the statement complained of was:

---

8 N.B. – this case was overturned but for different reasons.

9 Paragraph 27

(a) untrue;

(b) known by the maker of that statement to be untrue; and

(c) made with the intention of the defendant and court relying upon that untruth.

Fundamental

It is not enough for the claim to be dishonest. Establishing dishonesty is merely the first stage or a two-stage test.[10] The dishonesty must also be 'fundamental'.

The fullest explanation of the concept, and the one most often cited, is in _Gosling v (1) Hailo (2) Screwfix Direct (HHJ Moloney QC, Cambridge County Court, 29th April 2014)_.

Seeing as it is the case to which most Judges will turn, it worth recalling the facts and judgment in full.

10At least in relation to the concept as contained within the CPR. In Section 57 the third stage of the test is to consider whether or not there is any 'substantial injustice' to the claimant in making such a finding.

Mr. Gosling suffered a serious injury to his knee as a result of an accident involving a ladder manufactured by the first defendant, and sold to him by the second defendant. The claim for special damages came to approximately £39,000, £17,000 of which (i.e. just over 40%) was for future care, and another £40,000 of which was claimed on account of pain, suffering and loss of amenity.

The claimant reported to the defendant's medical expert that he suffered from almost constant knee pain, and that he still had to use one crutch in his hand. He reported that his problems were many, and included the fact that when he and his wife went shopping, he would have to wait in the car. He also made it clear within his witness statement that he frequently had cause to use a wheelchair.

The defendant obtained surveillance evidence that showed the claimant visiting a superstore. He and his wife walked around the store for just under an hour, during which time the claimant had no need for a crutch or support. He then drove to his medical examination with the second defendant's expert, Dr. Shaolin, and before entering the Hospital, he fetched his crutch from the back of the van and walked into Hospital with it.

It was during that interview that the claimant proceeded to tell Dr. Shaolin about all of the (alleged) problems mentioned above, *including* the fact that he would have to wait in the car whilst his wife went shopping.

The surveillance evidence was served and disclosed to both medical experts, who in their joint report concluded:

"(a) The claimant does not need to walk with a crutch;

(b) In general terms, the knee pain following a total knee replacement has two major causes: firstly, the diagnosis was not correct and there was no significant arthritis – this was not the case for Mr. Gosling. Secondly, that the patient has failed to rehabilitate their muscles properly. The surveillance videos show that this, also, is not correct.

Therefore, there is no evidence that Mr. Gosling has constant knee pain, except that he reports it. We are sure the court will take the inference that the disparity between the examination findings and the complaints that we found when doing the medical reports, and the surveillance video which suggests that there is no problem, is that Mr. Gosling is not being honest about his symptoms and problems."

The claimant continued with his claim but served a revised schedule of loss, abandoning the claim for future care in its entirety.

The claim against the first defendant was settled and the claim against the second defendant was discontinued. Despite that, the second defendant wished to pursue the claimant for an enforceable costs order, and made an application for a finding that the claim was fundamentally dishonest.

The claimant argued that even if the evidence obtained *was* evidence of exaggeration, then as a matter of law that did not make the claim *fundamentally* dishonest. As such, HHJ Moloney QC was forced to examine the meaning of the word '*fundamentally*'. The following passage has now been cited in numerous County Courts up and down the country:

> "*Of course, the term "fundamental" is used in various legal contexts that are of little assistance to us here. Dictionary definitions were produced and relied upon; for example, that which was fundamental was "of, or pertaining to, the basis or groundwork of something", "going to the root of the*

matter", "serving as the base or foundation", "essential or indispensable".

"*It appears to me that this phrase in the rules has to be interpreted purposively and contextually in the light of the context. This is, of course, the determination of whether the claimant is "deserving", as Jackson LJ put it, of the protection (from the costs liability that would otherwise fall on him) extended, for reasons of social policy, by the QOCS rules. It appears to me that when one looks at the matter in that way, one sees that what the rules are doing is distinguishing between two levels of dishonesty: dishonesty in relation to the claim which is not fundamental so as to expose such a claimant to costs liability, and dishonesty which is fundamental, so as to give rise to costs liability.* "*

"*The corollary term to "fundamental" would be a word with some such meaning as "incidental" or "collateral". Thus, a claimant should not be exposed to costs liability merely because he is shown to have been dishonest as to some collateral matter or perhaps as to some minor, self-contained head of damage. If, on the other hand, the dishonesty went to the root of either the whole of his claim or a substantial part of his claim, then it appears to me that it would be a fundamentally dishonest claim: a claim which depended as to a substantial or important part of itself upon dishonesty."[11]*

It was open to HHJ Moloney QC to define fundamental dishonesty as something that <u>only</u> went to the '*root*' or '*to the heart*' of the matter. This would include for example claims where injury was alleged where there was none, or that there was a collision when in fact there was not. In that instance, the dishonesty would evidently be fundamental.

However, as he explained, that would be too pure and narrow a view of the concept, and if such an interpretation was applied that would be to defeat the purpose of the provision – namely to deter frivolous or fraudulent claims. The dishonesty therefore need not necessarily go to either the root of liability or to the damages in their entirety. The concept would, it was held, also encompass claims where the dishonesty went to a '*substantial or important*' part of the claim.

The dishonesty in the case of *Gosling* was the claimant's complaint that he was suffering from serious ongoing pain and a lack of function in his knee. Taking a fairly broad brush

---

11 Paragraphs 43, 44 and 45

approach, the Judge came to the view that in monetary terms, approximately half of the claim could be attributed to the claimant's dishonesty, which constituted a *substantial* enough element for the claim to be held to be fundamentally dishonest.

As mentioned above, most Judges have adopted the above definition. As was explained in <u>*Menary v Darnton*</u>, there was nothing magic in the word fundamental. HHJ Hughes QC pointed towards the use of the same word in different contexts:

> "*In terms of ordinary language, the word 'fundamental' was given its classic definition for forensic purposes by Lord Upjohn in the well-known Suisse Atlantique case [1966] 2 All ER 61 at pages 85 to 86. I quote so far as is necessary for present purposes:*

> '*There is no magic in the words 'fundamental breach'; this expression is no more than a convenient shorthand expression for saying that a particular breach or breaches of contract by one party is or are such as to go to the root of the contract which entitles the other party to treat such breach or breaches as a repudiation of the whole contract.*

Whether such breach or breaches do constitute a funda-mental breach depends on the construction of the contract and on all the facts and circumstances of the case. A funda-mental term of a contract is a stipulation which the parties have agreed either expressly or by necessary implication or which the general law regards as a condition which goes to the root of the contract so that any breach of that term may at once and G without further reference to the facts and circumstances be regarded by the innocent party as a funda-mental breach.'"[12]

Similarly, in <u>Rayner v Raymond Brown Group Ltd (3rd August 2016, Oxford CC, HHJ Harris QC)</u> the Judge's approach was:

"… to direct myself that fundamental dishonesty within the meaning of CPR44 means a substantial and material dishonesty going to the heart of the claim – either liability or quantum or both – rather than peripheral exaggerations or embroidery, and it will be a question in fact and degree in each case. Both counsel have accepted that formula-tion."[13]

---

12 See paragraph 9 of Menary

13 Paragraph 10

A definition – summary

Taking the above together, in attempting to define fundamental dishonesty, the question one should ask is something along the lines of:

Is the claim either entirely or substantially based upon an untruth, of which the claimant knew, and upon which he/she intended the parties and court to rely?

The burden and standard of proof

The burden

He who avers must prove. It follows and should be obvious therefore that the person who alleges fundamental dishonesty is the person who must prove that that is the case.

The standard

The standard of proof is on the balance of probabilities. CPR 44.16 (and Section 57) makes that clear. That said, the guidance from Lord Nicholls in *In Re H and Others (Minors) [1996] A.C. 563*, is often cited (mistakenly) to be some type of departure from that standard.

Lord Nicholls opined that:

"*When assessing the probabilities the court will have in mind as a factor, to whatever extent is appropriate in the particular case, that the more serious the allegation the less likely it is that the event occurred and, hence, the stronger should be the evidence before the court concludes that the allegation is established on the balance of probability. . . .*

Although the result is much the same, this does not mean that where a serious allegation is in issue the standard of proof required is higher. It means only that the inherent probability or improbability of an event is itself a matter to be taken into account when weighing the probabilities and deciding whether, on balance, the event occurred. The more improbable the event, the stronger must be the evidence that it did occur before, on the balance of probability, its occurrence will be established. Ungoed-Thomas J expressed this neatly in In re Dellow's Will Trusts [1964] 1 WLR 451, 455: The more serious the allegation the more cogent is the evidence required to overcome the unlikelihood of what is alleged and thus to prove it."

Although that guidance still holds true and is often followed in the County Courts it is important to emphasise that this does not mean that there is a higher standard of proof. It simply means that the inherent improbability of a serious allegation (such as fraud) must be taken into account, *along with all the other factors in the case.*

The logic is that it is assumed that there is an inherent improbability that an individual will deliberately attempt to mislead the court for his or her own financial gain. It therefore will take more than mere inconsistencies to make a finding of dishonesty.

Some examples

None of the below (or above) examples are binding on a Judge as to when he or she should come to make a finding of fundamental dishonesty. However, they will hopefully serve to give a further flavour of what is required for such a finding to be made.

Stanton v Hunter (31st March 2017, Liverpool County Court, Recorder SA Hatfield QC)

The claimant was injured when he fell through the roof of an outhouse building onto the ground below on the defendant's farm. He sustained multiple fractures as a result.

Prior to the accident, the claimant was a taxi driver, and he had asserted within his particulars of claim that he had not returned to work since the accident and that he would not be able to return to work in the future. However, surveillance evidence uncovered the fact that he had worked for several days from January – March 2014, and on at least 133 occasions between September 2012 and 2015.

The claimant resiled from his claim that the accident had prevented him from working, conceding that he was doing some work, but not as much as he used to. He explained that the reason he had stated he was not working was that he was not making a profit, which was what he understood to be 'working'. He also spoke of his poor memory, difficulties with literacy and the time pressures he was under in signing off the documents that contained the false claims relating to earnings.

The Judge rejected the claimant's explanation for the changes.

Firstly, the concept of 'working' was a straightforward one.

Secondly, although there were complaints of pressure from the firm of solicitors that represented him previously, that was an averment that was not mentioned in any documents or statements of case. Neither was that averment supported by the evidence of the claimant's daughter, who worked in the personal injury field and assisted her father with documents such as the schedule etc. It was clear that the documents had been clearly explained to him.

Thirdly, the claimant's neuropsychologist gave evidence that he was confident that the claimant had at no point indicated anything other than he had not returned to work.

Fourthly, disclosure of the correspondence as between the claimant and his former solicitors demonstrated a record of *conspicuous propriety* on the part of the claimant's solicitor and counsel, which further disproved the claimant's aversions about being put under pressure by his solicitors.

As such, the claim was fundamentally dishonest.

Admans v Two Saints Ltd (24th June 2016, Swindon County Court, Recorder J Watson QC)

This was a manual handling claim that arose out of allegedly heavy lifting performed by the claimant on the 28th May 2012. The basic assertion repeated in the medical reports was that by the end of the day she was doubled over in pain and had been unable to work since the accident. Furthermore, it was said that she was suffering from a high level of disabling back pain and a loss of function '24/7'.

The defendant obtained surveillance evidence, and after disclosing the same, applied to have the claim struck out as fraudulent.

The video showed the claimant engaging normally with others, as well as closing up a shop without any limitations. This included carrying containers and pulling in clothing rails from outside. It also showed her driving to a convenience store and taking out cash from an ATM. The Judge found that, *'there is no hint in any of this sequence [of the video] of anything other than completely normal physical function.'*[14]

---

14 See paragraph 37

The video footage was entirely incompatible with the claimant's own descriptions of her disability. Furthermore, even though she had had over two months to formulate her response to the footage, she had failed to serve any evidence to support her case (she had been formerly represented by solicitors who by the time of the hearing had come off the record). Finally, the 'good day/bad day' explanation did not appear anywhere in her evidence or in her answers to Part 18 questions put by the defendant.

Dishonesty was therefore the only possible explanation for the discrepencies. That dishonesty had been maintained over an extended period and it had a fundamental impact on the assessment of the claim, which was struck out.

Zurich Insurance PLC v Bain (4th June 2015, Newcastle Upon Tyne County Court, HHJ Freedman)

The accident occurred on the 30th October 2012 when the claimant was involved in a minor collision. As the defendant's driver reversed, he collided with the near side front of the claimant's vehicle passing behind.

It was claimed that the claimant suffered from moderate back pain for eight weeks, causing him to be uncomfortable whilst driving and which restricted his ability to garden. It was claimed that there was no pre-existing symptomology. The Judge at first instance found that the claimant had suffered no injury at all, but declined to make a finding of fundamental dishonesty.

Unsurprisingly, that decision was overturned. If there was a positive finding that there was no injury (rather than the injury was simply not proved) then the claimant had made a false assertion that propped up the entire claim. Such an example was the epitome of fundamental dishonesty.

Rayner v Brown (3rd August 2016, Oxford County Court, HHJ Harris QC)

The claimants alleged that they were involved in a road traffic accident due to a lorry being driven negligently by the defendant. The defendant produced evidence that the said lorry was not in the area of the accident at the time, and the same seems to have been impressed upon counsel for the claimant prior to trial. The claimant sought leave to adjourn and amend (which was dismissed), and so counsel sought instructions. Upon return he indicated his wish to discontinue and by this stage the claimants had left court. The first instance Judge did not make a finding of fundamental dishonesty in relation to the accident (which was surprising), but instead made a finding in relation to the severity of the injuries claimed, finding that they had either been non-existent or substantially exaggerated. The claimant appealed, arguing that the Judge had insufficient evidence upon which to base such a finding.

The appeal was dismissed. There was evidence from an engineer or assessor, who described the damage to the vehicle as '*light*'. Despite that, the evidence of the first claimant in her witness statement described the impact as '*heavy*'.

Whilst that was not sufficient in itself, both claimants also said that they were suffering from pain within a few hours that they rated as 7/10 on the visual analogue scale. Despite that, the first claimant failed to visit her GP. The second claimant *did* visit her GP, but failed to mention anything at all about the accident.

Finally, the prognoses for both claimants was six months, yet they were still complaining of symptoms at 12 months. Taken *together* that was sufficient evidence for the Judge to make a finding of fundamental dishonesty in relation to the alleged injuries.

Meadows v La Tasca (16th June 2016, Manchester CC, HHJ Hodge QC)

The claimant alleged that she fell whilst at the defendant's restaurant and suffered injuries as a result. The claim was dismissed. In relation to the claimant's evidence the first instance Judge held:[15]

> "*I am not satisfied that Miss Meadows slipped while she was leaving La Tasca restaurant on 14 January 2014, and on that basis I must dismiss the claim. The reason that I have reached that conclusion is because to accept that Miss Meadows fell in the way that she claims would have me believe what Miss Meadows and Mrs. McGrath told me in their evidence. Their evidence is so riddled with inconsistencies, both internally and in relation to the*

---

15 See paragraph 5 of the Judgment on appeal

inconsistencies between the evidence of Miss Meadows and Mrs. McGrath, which, when I test that against objective contemporaneous evidence, has led me to conclude that I cannot rely on anything that they tell me in relation to the circumstances giving rise to the claim."

The Judge went on to list 14 to 15 inconsistencies that he had identified, and concluded that he could not believe that the accident happened, and on that basis, he found the claimant to be fundamentally dishonest. The claimant appealed.

The appeal was allowed. The Judge had not addressed the inherent improbability of the claimant and her witness getting together in order to manufacture a claim. That was important since that was the conclusion that the Judge had effectively reached. There was nothing to suggest that the claimant and the witness were not *'thoroughly honest individuals'* who had not been involved in this sort of thing before. The Judge had fallen into the trap of thinking that there was a binary choice between thinking that the accident did occur or that it did not occur. The third option (which he should have found) was of course that the claimant had simply failed to prove her claim.

Conclusion

There is no appellate authority on the precise meaning of fundamental dishonesty. However, whilst a precise definition might be of some help, it seems that most Judges have not struggled too much with semantics.

Nevertheless, and by way of some type of 'check list' against which it may be helpful to assess claims, the party alleging fundamental dishonesty should be able to show that the claimant/counter-claimant:

(a) Made an untrue statement (not just something that was not believed);

(b) The maker of that statement knew it to be untrue (or did not actively believe in its truth);

(c) That the statement was intended to be relied upon by the parties and the court;

(d) The statement went to the root of the claim, *or* to a substantial *or* important part of it.

CHAPTER FOUR
FUNDAMENTAL DISHONESTY
IN PRACTICE

Tips for assessing fundamental dishonesty

Assessing the credibility of a witness can often be a difficult task, especially given the general fallibility of the human memory.[1] However, in alleging dishonesty, one is not merely alleging that the claimant's evidence is unreliable. One is seeking to establish that it is a deliberate attempt to mislead, which is a far more difficult task, as proved to be the case in _Miley v Friends Life Ltd [2017] EWHC 2415 QB_.

In _Miley_ the issue was whether or not the claimant was entitled to claim payments from the defendant under an income protection scheme. His case was that he was unable to do his job because of CFS (Chronic Fatigue Syndrome). The defendant alleged that the claimant was 'faking it' or at least exaggerating his symptoms, and counter-claimed for the sums already paid.

---

1 For an explanation of the problems with human memory see Mr. Justice Leggatt's guidance at paragraphs 16 – 23 of Gestmin v (1) Credit Suisse (UK) Ltd (2) Credit Suisse Securities (Europe) Ltd [2013] EWHC 3560 (Comm)

Several issues arose in that case that frequently arise in other cases where some type of dishonesty is alleged.

Discrepencies

In *Miley* the defendant obtained covert surveillance which showed several discrepencies with his evidence.

Firstly, it was said that he had failed to mention to the medical assessor that he had been on a break to Southampton, contrary to the fact that he had told him (the assessor) that when he went on holiday his symptoms were made worse.

Secondly, the claimant had claimed in an Employment Appeal that he could only manage to wear a tracksuit (unless necessary to wear something else), whereas the surveillance showed him 6 months later in normal clothes, functioning normally.

Thirdly, he had claimed that he was not earning any income between 2011 and 2013, but failed to disclose that he owned shares. It was said by the defendant that such shares should have been included in the form as a declared income.

None of these discrepencies were irrelevant, but none of them were sufficiently '*stark or contradictory*' enough to support an allegation of dishonesty. Indeed, each one of them was (in principle) explicable. *Meadows v La Tasca* (above) was a similar such case in that the Judge held that mere inconsistencies were not enough to prove dishonesty.

In assessing whether a claim is dishonest, one should ask whether or not a discrepancy is sufficiently '*stark or contradictory*' to support an allegation of fundamental dishonesty.

Furthermore, in alleging dishonesty, it is not good enough to rely or point towards 'gaps' in the claimant's evidence.

Again, in *Miley* for example, the defendant complained that the claimant had taken frequent holidays, both at home and abroad, which would have required a certain level of stamina contrary to his general condition. However, the claimant was never asked about what he *did* on those holidays. The fact that he went abroad when the evidence wasn't *necessarily* inconsistent, since it wasn't clear as to what he participated in whilst actually on those holidays. One cannot seek to rely on mere inferences when alleging dishonesty.

Motive

Motive is unlikely to be sufficient in and of itself to support an allegation of dishonesty.

Other witnesses

The evidence of other witnesses is likely to have an impact on any assessment of dishonesty, even if those witnesses are not independent. In <u>Miley</u>, the claimant was supported by his wife, his mother and close friends. Although '*love and affection breed loyalty*',[2] the defendant's case meant that they would have to be: *either* complicit in the claimant's fraud *or* the claimant would have had to have kept a sufficiently consistent and credible portrayal of serious disability to fool all of them. Both of those hypotheses were improbable.

Whether one is representing either a claimant or a defendant, one should not dismiss the evidence of witnesses simply

---

2 See paragraph 62 of Miley

because they are either family or friends. Such evidence is likely to be given some weight.

Are the choices binary?

It is worth asking whether the two factual scenarios present a binary choice.

For example, in *Creech v (1) Apple security group ltd (2) Severn valley railway (holdings) plc (3) Irvin leisure entertainments Ltd. (25th March 2015, Telford County Court, District Judge Rogers)* the claimant alleged that he had tripped on a pile of matting on a railway station platform. The matts were formerly part of a temporary ice rink. The defendant adduced evidence (accepted at trial) that everything had been cleared away and that there was no chance that anything could have been left behind.

The Judge accepted the defendant's evidence and as such, the claimant was found to be fundamentally dishonest. Either the matting was there or it was not. There was no room for *'misremembering'* or *'unconscious bias'*.

When assessing one's own case it might therefore be worth asking whether or not the Judge will be faced with a similar 'black or white' option. If so, then the risk of a finding of fundamental dishonesty may be greater, as there will be no third way for the Judge to follow come trial.

Irrelevant considerations – 'not the type'

Where dishonesty is alleged, and when assessing the prospects of success, several factors in assessing prospects are often taken into account that should not be. One such factor is the claimant's background. For example, it is often said that the claimant does not seem like the dishonest 'type' to be making up or exaggerating a claim.

This however, is to confuse *the claim* with *the claimant*. The two are very different, and it is worth remembering that the claimant's background or profession should play no part in one's risk assessment.

For example, in *Sikand* (below), which was a particularly egregious example of dishonesty, the claimant was training to be a Solicitor. In *Zurich v Bain* the claimant was an ambulance driver, yet had brought a claim for injuries which was found to be entirely false. It is worth therefore remembering that even honest people can (in the words of HHJ Freedman in _Zurich_) '_succumb to the temptation_' to make a claim when pressure is exerted upon them by claims management companies.

Irrelevant considerations – apparent candour

Another consideration that often plays a part in the analysis of prospects (but should not) is the apparent candour of the claimant. For example, it might be said that if he or she has volunteered some information that is detrimental to the value of the claim, then surely, they cannot be dishonest? Indeed, it is often asked rhetorically: if the claim was exaggerated then why proffer that information at all?

Whilst every case turns on its own facts, hopefully most will be able to see the fallacy in that logic. Just because the claimant has been honest about x does not mean he or she is being honest about y.

This point was made in _Menary_, where the claimant had been involved in two accidents – one that was the subject of the claim and another one prior to that. When the claimant visited the medical expert for the purposes of his claim he disclosed that he had been in a prior accident and disclosed that he had suffered lower back symptoms as a result. The submission was made that the disclosure of the prior incident showed that the claimant had nothing to hide. If the claim was fraudulent then why would the claimant disclose his medical history?

That submission was rejected. Not only was the submission a logical fallacy, but in many cases it may well be that (as the Judge found on appeal in _Menary_) the claimant disclosed that history precisely because he knew that it would come out in any event.

Other practical tips

Put the claimant on notice

It is astonishing how often claimants are not properly warned about the consequences of bringing an exaggerated or fraudulent claim. Those consequences are severe. Not only will the claimant be faced with potentially having to pay the defendant's costs (which may well not be covered by either ATE or BTE), but they may well be committed for contempt of court. Such warnings can often focus the mind when recollecting events and injuries.

Pleadings

Where there is sufficient evidence to do so, fundamental dishonesty should be pleaded within the defence, along with any particulars of dishonesty (i.e. what it is about the claim that is said to be dishonest).

If the evidence of dishonesty materialises after the service of the defence, steps should be taken to amend the pleadings to plead fundamental dishonesty if possible.

Test the evidence

If there is suspicion of dishonesty, and especially if those suspicions have been raised or pleaded by the defendant, then a conference with the client (admittedly a rarity in lower value claims) is going to be invaluable.

Normally the costs (or at least disbursements) for holding a conference will be irrecoverable. However, where fundamental dishonesty is pleaded, the courts have been known (at least in the writer's experience) to on occasion award counsel's costs for the conference as a disbursement that was '*necessary due to a particular feature of the dispute*' (see CPR 45.12 (C)).

Even if those costs are not recoverable, it is worth thinking about whether or not it would be worth bearing the costs of a conference in any event, even if it is over the telephone, or if the solicitor is not present in person.

If such a conference goes ahead, then it should go without saying that that conference should be thorough and should take advantage of the chance to correct or clarify any inconsistencies in the evidence. There may still be time to look for further disclosure, or to file a supplementary witness statement. The conference may also be beneficial for exploring avenues that had not yet been explored.

Accurate pleadings and statements

It seems to have become a feature of low value fast track work that pleadings are sloppily drafted, and that witness statements are brief to the point of being almost entirely unhelpful. In that context statements of truth are often an afterthought.

However, since the advent of CPR 44.16 and Section 57, such documents should be seen as having greatly increased in importance. Whilst Judges often make allowances when claimants are cross-examined, in the writer's experience those allowances are becoming far less common. As the Judge in *Diamtekk v James (8th February 2016, Coventry County Court, HHJ Gregory)* emphasised:

> "*Litigation is not conducted in a vacuum. It is conducted through statements of the case which are intended to present the cases of the competing parties. It is important that those statements of case should be accurate and honest, and that is why they have to be verified by statements of truth.*"[3]

---

3 Paragraph 2

Summary

In assessing whether or not a claim is fundamentally dishonest, it is useful to remember:

- Discrepencies do not equate to dishonesty.

- Neither do gaps in the claimant's evidence.

- Witness evidence should not be dismissed simply because it is not 'independent'.

- One should look at whether the choice for the Judge is binary (i.e. are there only two options as to the events complained of?)

- The claimant's background should not be taken into account.

- Nor should any apparent candour.

- Those representing claimants should make them fully aware of the risks involved in being found to be fundamentally dishonest.

- Fundamental dishonesty must be pleaded as a defence where possible.

- Conferences with the claimant may be of benefit.

- Extreme care should be taken when drafting any document signed with a statement of truth.

CHAPTER FIVE
APPLICATIONS TO STRIKE OUT
AND SECTION 57

<u>Summers v Fairclough Homes Ltd [2012] UKSC 26</u> confirmed that the court has the power (in principle) to strike out a case as an abuse of process after the trial had concluded. However, as Lord Clarke explained, one needn't wait until the conclusion of proceedings before making that application:

> "...nothing in this judgment affects the correct approach in a case where an application is made to strike out a statement of case in whole or in part at an early stge. As the Court of Appeal put it in Masood v Zahoor at para 73 (set out above) in a passage with which we agree, one of the objects to be achieved by striking out a claim is to stop proceedings and prevent the further waste of precious resources on proceedings which the claimant has forfeited the right to have determined."[1]

The application to strike out can therefore be made at an interlocutory stage.

---

1 Paragraph 62

However, in practice succeeding in such an application can be difficult, since the court will be wary of taking such a draconian step. That was the case in _Alpha Rocks solicitors v Benjamin Oluwadare Alade [2015] EWCA Civ 685_, which although not a personal injury case, was still concerned with interlocutory strike out applications and fraud.

In that case, the claimant solicitors brought a claim for unpaid fees. The defendant client responded that the two bills presented to him for payment had been fraudulently exaggerated or misstated and therefore applied to strike out the whole claim. After considering the written evidence, the first instance Judge granted the application to strike out, holding that the solicitors were guilty of an abuse of process in bringing the claims for deliberately exaggerated fees. The solicitors appealed. Lord Justice Vos, giving the lead judgment commented:

> "_As Masood and Summers supra also demonstrate, striking out is available in such cases at an early stage in the proceedings, but only where a claimant is guilty of misconduct in relation to those proceedings which is so serious that it would be an affront to the court to permit him to continue to prosecute the claim, and where the claim_

should be struck out in order to prevent the further waste of precious resources on proceedings which the claimant has forfeited the right to have determined."[2]

"In my judgment, the court should exercise caution in the early stages of a case in striking out the entirety of a claim on the grounds that a part has been improperly or even fraudulently exaggerated. That is because of the draconian effect of so doing and the risk that, at a trial, events may appear less clear cut than they do at an interlocutory stage. The court is not easily affronted, and in my judgment the emphasis should be on the availability of fair trial of the issues between the parties. As CPR Part 3.4(2)(b) itself says, "[t]he court may strike out a statement of case if … the statement of case is an abuse of the court's process or is otherwise likely to obstruct the just disposal of the proceedings" (emphasis added)."[3]

Whilst it may be difficult to succeed on such strike out applications, that is not to say that it is necessarily impossible, and there are cases where the evidence will be overwhelming, as

---

2 Paragraph 21

3 Paragraph 22

was the case in *Sikand v CS Lounge and LA Fitness (11th July 2016, Mayor's and City of London Court, District Judge Avent).*

In that case, the claimant brought two claims for personal injuries after he was involved in two separate accidents. The first accident was on the 6th March 2012 when he allegedly injured himself whilst working for the first defendant. The second accident was on the 19th April 2012, when he further injured himself after the bench in the sauna he had been sitting on collapsed. In both cases liability was admitted.

A not insignificant claim was made for loss of earnings, it being alleged that the claimant was either unable to, or extremely restricted in, his ability to work. The future loss was not yet particularised, but by the time of the hearing the past loss of earnings came to the rather substantial sum of (approximately) £65,000.

Despite the claimant's alleged inability to work, his social media profiles (Twitter and LinkedIn) contained numerous references to working full time, and indeed, to working two jobs. The entries are too numerous to include[4] here but suffice

---

4 For a full list of the updates see paragraph 68 of the Judgment.

to say that his entire CV on LinkedIn was completely unin-
terrupted, and his twitter profile was full of posts such as:

*"16.05.2014 @rhaynukaa not bad when you consider
balancing the stresses of a business, 2 jobs, voluntary work
and family life lol - #soldier #committed"*

*"8.11.2014 Finally my working day is done!! Gym, trip to
Peckham & back, afternoon of paperwork, running a
restaurant & finally after 21 hours to bed."* and

*"19.12.2014 "Day job done, now on to job 2, which
means I miss the wk Xmas party and lastly flyering after I
finish wk!! #dedicated #law #partyatthetop."*

Finally, and as if that was not enough, the defendant also
obtained surveillance evidence showing the claimant going to
the gym and going running.

Taking all the evidence into account, and after comparing it
to the aversions that had been made in *both* schedules of loss
and the responses to Part 18 requests (all signed by statements
of truth) the Judge struck out the claim. He was of the view
that:

"There is no way round this for Mr. Sikand; it cannot be explained away other than being a deliberate and purposeful lie. It was clearly designed to dishonestly support his loss of earnings claim."[5]

Furthermore, not only was there no way around it, but also:

"Mr. Sikand had the opportunity to admit, recognise and apologise for his dishonest conduct in his second witness statement but, far from doing so, he not only maintained the fiction which he had previously advanced but singularly failed to explain how he had come to sign statements of truth which were clearly incorrect. He also, extraordinarily, sought to suggest that his Twitter account was not relevant and to minimise his conduct; there was no acknowledgement that he had done anything wrong at all."[6]

He concluded:

"The concept of whether it would be 'just' can also be measured in more principled terms particularly since the

---

5 Paragraph 127

6 Paragraph 135

*reforms of Jackson LJ. It is not only 'just' but also propor-
tionate that fraudulent or dishonest claims should be rooted
out where appropriate and that litigants and potential litigants should fully understand that such an approach to the
litigation process will not be tolerated. Whether a case is
then struck out or not will obviously depend upon the
extent of the misconduct involved. However, Miss Crapper
was right to mention the prevailing winds that are blowing
against fraudulent claims.*

*There are those rare cases where the consequences of telling
untruths before trial, where they pervade and permeate
across the case generally or are so central to the issues, are so
serious and irremediable that they must, in my view,
contaminate the remainder of the evidence and the case.
The outcome is that the whole case becomes tainted and the
claimant forfeits his right to a trial. This is one such case
and, accordingly, I conclude that it is just and proportionate that the cases which Mr. Sikand has brought,
against both CLS and LAF, should be struck out."[7]*

---

7 Paragraphs 161 and 162.

Summary

As _Sikand_ illustrates, in order to succeed on a strike out application, the evidence of the dishonesty will need to be particularly strong. Where there is any doubt, a Judge is likely to decide that such matters should be heard at trial.

CHAPTER SIX
DISCONTINUANCE

Discontinuance generally

Under *CPR 38.2 (1)*, a claimant may discontinue all or part of a claim at *any* time, subject to some exceptions, two of which are relevant for the purposes of personal injury cases.

The first exception is that if there has been an interim payment, then the claimant must obtain permission from the defendant or the court (CPR 38.2 (2) (b)). This may be the case for example in a liability admitted claim where the defendant has already made a modest interim payment.

The second exception is that where there is more than one claimant, the permission of *all* the other claimants must be obtained before one discontinues (see CPR 38.2 (c)). This would be applicable in, for example, passenger claims.

As far as the procedure is concerned, in order to formally discontinue, a notice of discontinuance needs to be filed and served (CPR 38.3 (1)). The notice must state that it has been served upon every other party (CPR 38.3 (2)), and insofar as consent is required, a copy of the necessary consent must be attached to the notice also (CPR 38.3 (3)).

Discontinuance and fundamental dishonesty

PD 44 12.4 (c) states that:

> "*Where the claimant has served a notice of discontinuance, the court may direct that issues arising out of an allegation that the claim was fundamentally dishonest be determined notwithstanding that the notice has not been set aside pursuant to rule 38.4.*"

The rules do not prescribe what test should be applied on an application that the issue of fundamental dishonesty be heard, or the type of evidence that would be required. Instead, the practice direction gives the court a wide and general discretion, meaning that the court must exercise its powers in accordance with the overriding objective, which will include having regard to proportionality. It is likely however that any application is going to have to be supported by '*stark and contradictory*' evidence of dishonesty. Relying on inferences and innuendo alone is unlikely to be sufficient to persuade a Judge to grant the application for a hearing.

Furthermore, the guidance given by HHJ Gosnell in _Rouse v Aviva Insurance Limited (15th January 2016, Bradford County Court)_ is also of some assistance as to the other factors the court may consider when hearing such an application:

> "_If I reach the conclusion that there may have to be a hearing at which parties can give evidence, I think it must be right that where the claimant does not give evidence or does not proffer any reason for the decision to discontinue, then the defendant can invite the court to draw an adverse inference.._"[1]

Proportionality is also likely to be a key factor:

> "_Take this case, for example. The defendant says that it has incurred costs of £11,293.36 which, leaving aside the fact that that might well be reduced on a summary assessment, it is a substantial sum of money. What would be the costs of having a somewhat limited enquiry as to whether this was a fundamentally dishonest claim? The answer is it would_

---

1 Paragraph 4 B

be, probably, roughly the same in this case as the costs in a fast track trial because of the fact that, perhaps in this case, it would be helpful to the claimant for him to give evidence and his driver and it may be helpful for the defendant's witnesses to give evidence although I am not convinced in this case that would be necessary. I have got to say that if the Rules say that the defendant can seek a direction that the claimant is fundamentally dishonest - and there is going to be some sort of fair procedure for that to happen - it would not necessarily be disproportionate for, perhaps, £2,000 to be spent at a three-hour hearing to determine whether there was fundamental dishonesty when the sum of £11,293.36 is at stake. "[2]

Summary

Whilst there is no *requirement* within the rules for the evidence to be of a certain 'strength', it is inevitable that the defendant will need to establish that there is a *prima facie* case of dishonesty, supported by clear and convincing evidence. It is unlikely that the court will allow for there to be a hearing

---

2 Paragraph 5 C

on the basis of inference and innuendo, in the hope that something 'comes out in the wash' in cross examination.

Secondly, in considering making an application to try the issue of fundamental dishonesty, it is worth assessing (as the Judge did in _Rouse_) what stage the proceedings are at and what costs have been incurred thus far. The question should be asked: is it proportionate to proceed with a hearing?

Finally, if the court is to hear the issue of fundamental dishonesty then it is almost inevitable that a hearing will be required. It is only fair that met with such a serious allegation, the claimant should have the opportunity to correct the record. Although the claimant need not necessarily have to be present[3], it would usually be highly inadvisable to not appear.

---

3 Indeed, _Rouse_ was decided in the claimants' absence.

CHAPTER SEVEN
COSTS CONSEQUENCES

Indemnity costs

Having found the claim to have been fundamentally dishonest, the court may award the defendant's costs to be assessed on the indemnity basis. In making that decision the court will have reference not only to the overriding objective but it must also have reference to the factors it is obliged to consider, namely:

CPR 44.2 (4)

(a) the conduct of all the parties;

(b) whether a party has succeeded on part of its case, even if that party has not been wholly successful; and

(c) any admissible offer to settle made by a party which is drawn to the court's attention, and which is not an offer to which costs consequences under Part 36 apply.

(5) The conduct of the parties includes —

(a) conduct before, as well as during, the proceedings and in particular the extent to which the parties followed the Practice Direction – Pre-Action Conduct or any relevant pre-action protocol;

(b) whether it was reasonable for a party to raise, pursue or contest a particular allegation or issue;

(c) the manner in which a party has pursued or defended its case or a particular allegation or issue; and

(d) whether a claimant who has succeeded in the claim, in whole or in part, exaggerated its claim.

The discretion to award indemnity costs is deliberately wide, and little guidance has been offered to the courts. The only real requirement is that the that the conduct complained of must take the case '*out of the norm*'. See *Excelsior Commercial & Industrial Holdings Ltd v Salisbury Hamer Aspden & Johnston (Costs)[2002] EWCA Civ 879*):

"This court can do no more than draw attention to the width of the discretion of the trial judge and re-emphasise the point that has already been made that, before an

indemnity order can be made, there must be some conduct or some circumstance which takes the case out of the norm."[1]

Whilst there is no specific guidance, traditionally, where dishonesty or an abuse of process is involved, it is difficult to envisage a case where costs would *not* be awarded on the indemnity basis. (See for example *Caliendo v Mischon De Reya unreported (Ch) 14 March 2016* – a professional negligence claim, where Mr. Justice Arnold had found that the claim relied upon a premise that the claimant knew to be false and so awarded costs on the indemnity basis).

Wasted costs orders

Indemnity costs are not the only consequence of fundamental dishonesty. It is worth remembering that should the claimant be unable to pay the costs of the defendant (which may well often be the case) then there may be reason for the defendant to apply for a wasted costs order against the claimant's solicitors.

---

1 Lord Woolf in *Excelsior* at paragraph 32

The power to make an order for wasted costs exists under Section 51 (6) of the Senior Courts Act 1982. The test is set out at paragraph 5.5 of the practice direction to Part 46 and is as follows:

5.5. It is appropriate for the court to make a wasted costs order against a legal representative, only if –

(a) the legal representative has acted improperly, unreasonably or negligently;

(b) the legal representative's conduct has caused a party to incur unnecessary costs, or has meant that costs incurred by a party prior to the improper, unreasonable or negligent act or omission have been wasted;

(c) it is just in all the circumstances to order the legal representative to compensate that party for the whole or part of those costs.

In most cases it is likely that an application for wasted costs will be dismissed since the claimant's solicitors are perfectly entitled to rely on their client's version of events.

That said, where fundamental dishonesty is proved, the evidence of dishonesty may be so compelling so as to justify a finding that the funding arrangement should have been terminated and that the solicitors should have come off the record, since to continue the claim in such circumstances would be an abuse of process.

That was the case in *Thompson v (1) Go North East and (2) Bott and Co Solicitors (30th August 2016, Sunderland County Court, District Judge Charnock-Neal)*.

In that case, the claimant brought proceedings against the first defendant, alleging that he was injured whilst travelling on a bus owned and operated by the defendant. He claimed that at the time of the accident he was standing up. That was the account given also to the medical expert who had initially supported the claim. Although breach of duty was admitted, the rest of the claim was denied.

After confirming the identity of the claimant, the defendant disclosed the CCTV footage from the bus at the time of the accident. The footage showed the claimant sitting down, and not standing up as alleged. Despite that fact, the claim was issued and proceeded almost until trial, even though the account given (as per the particulars of claim and the claimant's witness statement) were directly contradicted by the CCTV footage that had been disclosed already.

As well as finding that the claimant himself had been fundamentally dishonest and should therefore pay the defendant's costs, the court also made an order for wasted costs against his former solicitors. The Judge held that:

"On the balance of probabilities, the Respondent acted improperly, or rather failed to act in February 2015 by not sending the Defendant's CCTV evidence to the doctor at that time. With the benefit of hindsight, the doctor would have given the same answers to the questions put to him earlier if he had been shown the CCTV evidence earlier. No explanation for this was given in the Claimant's witness statement, drafted by the Respondent or in Mr. Spain's witness statement. By October that year the Respondent issued proceedings for the Claimant knowing the version of events in the Particulars of Claim contradicted the Claimant's version given to Dr. Bratch. That was improper and could be negligent. In March 2016 the Respondent filed on behalf of the Claimant a witness statement with a different explanation of the mechanism of injury despite the

evidence of the CCTV. I find that that was also improper conduct."[2]

There have been other unreported County Court decisions of Judges making wasted costs orders in similar circumstances.

Sanctions for misconduct

An application for wasted costs may well be accompanied by an application for costs due to misconduct. That application would be made under *CPR 44.11* –

(1) The court may make an order under this rule where –

(a)...

(b) it appears to the court that the conduct of a party or that party's legal representative, before or during the proceedings or in the assessment proceedings, was unreasonable or improper.

(2) Where paragraph (1) applies, the court may –

---

2 Paragraph 33

(a) ...

(b) order the party at fault or that party's legal represen-tative to pay costs which that party or legal representative has caused any other party to incur.

(3) Where –

(a) the court makes an order under paragraph (2) against a legally represented party; and

(b) the party is not present when the order is made, the party's legal representative must notify that party in writing of the order no later than 7 days after the legal represen-tative receives notice of the order.

<u>44 PD 11.2</u> states that:

Conduct which is unreasonable or improper includes steps which are calculated to prevent or inhibit the court from furthering the overriding objective.

Within the context of personal injury claims and funda-mental dishonesty, the type of conduct that would be sufficient to make an order under CPR 44.11 is likely to be similar conduct to that which would be necessary to make a wasted costs order. It will therefore make little difference in practice under which provision the application is made, but it would be sensible to make that application under both provisions.

Summary

In summary:

- Indemnity costs against the claimant will almost certainly follow after a finding of fundamental dishonesty.

- The solicitor representing the claimant may run the risk of having a wasted costs order against him/her if the evidence of dishonesty is obvious.

MORE BOOKS BY
LAW BRIEF PUBLISHING

A selection of our other titles available now:

'Practical Mediation: A Guide for Mediators, Advocates, Advisers, Lawyers, and Students in Civil, Commercial, Business, Property, Workplace, and Employment Cases' by Jonathan Dingle with John Sephton
'A Comparative Guide to Standard Form Construction and Engineering Contracts' by Jon Close
'A Practical Guide to Compliance for Personal Injury Firms Working With Claims Management Companies' by Paul Bennett
'A Practical Guide to the Landlord and Tenant Act 1954: Commercial Tenancies' by Richard Hayes & David Sawtell
'A Practical Guide to Personal Injury Claims Involving Animals' by Jonathan Hand
'A Practical Guide to Psychiatric Claims in Personal Injury' by Liam Ryan
'Introduction to the Law of Community Care in England and Wales' by Alan Robinson

'A Practical Guide to Dog Law for Owners and Others' by Andrea Pitt

'Ellis and Kevan on Credit Hire, 5th Edition' by Aidan Ellis & Tim Kevan

'RTA Allegations of Fraud in a Post-Jackson Era: The Handbook, 2nd Edition' by Andrew Mckie

'A Practical Guide to Holiday Sickness Claims' by Andrew Mckie & Ian Skeate

'RTA Personal Injury Claims: A Practical Guide Post-Jackson' by Andrew Mckie

'On Experts: CPR35 for Lawyers and Experts' by David Boyle

'An Introduction to Personal Injury Law' by David Boyle

'A Practical Guide to Running Housing Disrepair and Cavity Wall Claims' by Andrew Mckie, Ian Skeate, Simon Redfearn

'A Practical Guide to Claims Arising From Accidents Abroad and Travel Claims' by Andrew Mckie & Ian Skeate

'A Practical Guide to Cosmetic Surgery Claims' by Dr Victoria Handley

'A Practical Guide to Chronic Pain Claims' by Pankaj Madan

'A Practical Guide to Marketing for Lawyers' by Catherine Bailey & Jennet Ingram
'The No Nonsense Solicitors' Practice: A Guide To Running Your Firm' by Bettina Brueggemann
'Baby Steps: A Guide to Maternity Leave and Maternity Pay' by Leah Waller
'The Queen's Counsel Lawyer's Omnibus: 20 Years of Cartoons from the Times 1993-2013' by Alex Steuart Williams

These books and more are available to order online direct from the publisher at www.lawbriefpublishing.com, where you can also read free sample chapters. For any queries, contact us on 0844 587 2383 or mail@lawbriefpublishing.com.

Our books are also usually in stock at www.amazon.co.uk with free next day delivery for Prime members, and at good legal bookshops such as Hammicks and Wildy & Sons.

We are regularly launching new books in our series of practical day-to-day practitioners' guides. Visit our website and join our free newsletter to be kept informed and to receive special offers, free chapters, etc.

You can also follow us on Twitter at:

www.twitter.com/lawbriefpub

24634915R00062

Printed in Great Britain
by Amazon